Mastering G. ⌐ ⌐
The Future of
Artificial Intelligence
in Your Hands

Unlock GPT-4's Capabilities, Ethical

Insights, and Proven Strategies for

Next-Level Productivity and Innovation

Lena Fairford

TABLE OF CONTENT

Introduction

The world we live in today is defined by rapid technological advances, and one of the most remarkable breakthroughs has been the development of artificial intelligence. At the forefront of this revolution is GPT-4, a language model that not only redefines what machines can do but also offers a new way of thinking about how humans and technology can work together. This powerful tool is quickly transforming industries, solving problems, and creating opportunities that were once unimaginable.

From revolutionizing customer service with intelligent chatbots to helping creatives and businesses streamline their operations, GPT-4 is already becoming an essential part of our daily lives.

Artificial intelligence, particularly language models like GPT-4, is no longer a futuristic concept; it's a present-day reality that is already having a profound effect on sectors ranging from healthcare and education to marketing, entertainment, and beyond.

The impact of AI is pervasive, shaping how we communicate, solve complex problems, and even make decisions. Its ability to understand and generate human-like text opens up endless possibilities for improving processes, enhancing creativity, and driving innovation. GPT-4, in particular, has raised the bar by not just responding to prompts but generating sophisticated, contextually aware text, making it a powerful tool for both businesses and individuals alike.

In this book, you will explore the full potential of GPT-4. We will start with the basics, helping you understand what GPT-4 is and how it works, before diving deeper into the numerous ways you can leverage its capabilities.

Whether you're an aspiring developer, a business professional, or a creative person looking to explore new frontiers, this guide will take you through every essential aspect of GPT-4, from its architecture to its ethical considerations. You'll learn how to fine-tune GPT-4 for specific tasks, integrate it into your workflows, and troubleshoot common issues. Along the way, you will gain valuable insights into how AI can be used responsibly, ensuring that you harness its power ethically and effectively.

By the end of this book, whether you're just starting or already have experience with AI, you will have a comprehensive understanding of GPT-4 and its applications. You'll walk away not only with technical knowledge but also with practical strategies for using GPT-4 to solve real-world challenges and open up new opportunities.

Embrace this transformative technology and take the first step toward mastering GPT-4—it's more than just an AI tool; it's your gateway to the future of innovation.

Chapter 1: Understanding GPT-4 – The Core of Modern AI

What is GPT-4?

The emergence of GPT-4 marks a significant milestone in the world of artificial intelligence. This tool, developed by OpenAI, represents a leap forward in natural language processing capabilities, enabling machines to better understand and generate human-like language. GPT-4 is the fourth iteration of the "Generative Pretrained Transformer" series, a type of machine learning model designed to generate text based on the input it receives.

It has been trained on an enormous dataset of text from books, websites, and other sources, which helps it produce responses that are contextually relevant and grammatically correct.

GPT-4 builds upon the work done in previous versions, including GPT-3, by refining its architecture and expanding its capabilities. The model's core function is to predict the next word in a sequence of words, using the vast amount of information it has absorbed during training.

What sets GPT-4 apart is its ability to generate more coherent, contextually aware, and nuanced responses. This is due to the increase in the number of parameters—millions or even billions of variables that influence how GPT-4 generates its text. These parameters are what allow GPT-4 to simulate a deeper understanding of language, making it an incredibly powerful tool for a wide variety of applications, from content creation to problem-solving.

The real power of GPT-4 lies in how it uses its training data to adapt to new situations. It doesn't just produce pre-programmed responses; instead, it generates text that is tailored to the context of the input, making its outputs feel more intuitive and human-like. Whether you're asking a simple question or requesting a detailed analysis, GPT-4 can provide an answer that matches the tone and complexity of the prompt, creating a seamless interaction that mimics human conversation.

How GPT-4 Works

At the heart of GPT-4's impressive capabilities is its underlying architecture: a transformer neural network. This model is based on the principles of deep learning, which is designed to simulate the way the human brain processes information. The transformer model excels at handling sequences of data, such as language, by using self-attention mechanisms to weigh the importance of each word in a sentence. This allows GPT-4 to process and understand context better than previous models.

The training process for GPT-4 involves feeding it large amounts of text data, allowing it to learn the statistical relationships between words, sentences, and even paragraphs. This process is known as "pretraining" and forms the foundation for GPT-4's ability to generate text. During pretraining, GPT-4 analyzes millions of examples to learn language patterns, syntax, and structure. Once this training is complete, GPT-4 can be fine-tuned for specific tasks, such as writing essays, answering questions, or generating code.

The architecture is built around layers of interconnected neurons, similar to how the human brain works. These neurons process input data by learning to identify patterns and relationships between various elements of the data. When you input a prompt into GPT-4, the model's parameters are activated to generate an output based on the patterns it has learned.

This process occurs incredibly fast, enabling GPT-4 to respond to a wide variety of prompts in real-time.

One of the key innovations in GPT-4 is its ability to handle a much larger amount of data and more complex tasks compared to earlier models. It can process longer sequences of text, maintain better coherence across longer passages, and generate outputs that are more aligned with the context in which they are used. This makes GPT-4 more versatile and capable of tackling a broader range of applications, from customer service chatbots to content generation and even data analysis.

GPT-4 vs. Other AI Models

When comparing GPT-4 to previous iterations like GPT-3 or other prominent AI models such as BERT and T5, several key differences stand out. GPT-4 improves upon GPT-3 in multiple ways, most notably in its scale and efficiency. While GPT-3 was already a massive model with 175 billion parameters, GPT-4 boasts an even larger number, enabling it to generate more accurate and contextually appropriate text. The increased size allows GPT-4 to have a deeper understanding of language and adapt more effectively to various types of prompts, making it far more reliable in complex tasks.

Another key difference between GPT-4 and GPT-3 lies in its ability to maintain coherence in longer text generations. GPT-3 often struggled with maintaining logical consistency in longer passages, sometimes generating outputs that veered off-topic or became nonsensical. GPT-4, however, has a more refined understanding of context, allowing it to produce more coherent, consistent, and accurate text over extended conversations or writings.

Comparing GPT-4 to other models like BERT and T5 highlights GPT-4's superiority in generating text, as opposed to just understanding it. BERT (Bidirectional Encoder Representations from Transformers) and T5 (Text-to-Text Transfer Transformer) are excellent at tasks such as sentiment analysis, question answering, and summarization, where the goal is to interpret existing text.

However, GPT-4's primary strength is its ability to generate new text based on a prompt, making it the go-to model for applications like creative writing, content generation, and dialogue creation. While BERT and T5 are focused on comprehension and classification tasks, GPT-4 can excel in creative and generative tasks, making it a more versatile choice for many industries.

In addition to its size and generative capabilities, GPT-4 outperforms its predecessors in its handling of nuances in language. The model's improved capacity for understanding context means that it can process more sophisticated prompts and provide answers that better reflect the complexities of the questions asked. Whether you're requesting a simple fact or seeking a detailed analysis, GPT-4 is able to provide a more comprehensive and insightful response than earlier models, making it an invaluable tool for a wide array of industries and applications.

Chapter 2: The Power of GPT-4 – Unlocking its Full Potential

Real-World Applications of GPT-4

The potential of GPT-4 spans across a wide array of industries, providing practical solutions that enhance productivity, creativity, and business operations. In content creation, GPT-4 stands out by producing human-like text that can be used for blogs, social media posts, articles, and more. This capability allows businesses to scale their content creation efforts without sacrificing quality. Whether you need to generate marketing copy, write product descriptions, or craft technical content, GPT-4 can handle it all with remarkable efficiency and accuracy.

For businesses aiming to improve their online presence, GPT-4's ability to generate engaging, brand-appropriate content is invaluable.

Another significant application of GPT-4 is in customer service. With the rise of AI-driven chatbots, GPT-4 has become an integral tool for enhancing customer interaction. Traditional chatbots often rely on basic scripted responses, but GPT-4 takes customer service to a new level by delivering more contextually aware and accurate answers. It can handle a wide range of customer queries, from simple questions to more complex troubleshooting tasks, all while maintaining a natural and conversational tone. By integrating GPT-4 into their customer support systems, businesses can provide 24/7 service, reduce wait times, and improve customer satisfaction.

GPT-4 also excels in data analysis. Traditionally, data analysts have spent hours sifting through raw data, looking for trends and insights.

GPT-4 simplifies this process by generating summaries of large datasets, offering actionable insights in plain language. This is particularly useful for non-technical stakeholders who may not be familiar with complex data analysis techniques. GPT-4 can be used to analyze customer feedback, sales data, or even large volumes of unstructured text, making it an essential tool for businesses looking to make data-driven decisions.

Machine translation is another area where GPT-4 makes a significant impact. While traditional translation tools are often limited by their inability to understand context, GPT-4 excels in providing more accurate and natural translations. Its ability to process and generate text in multiple languages means it can be used to translate everything from business documents to real-time conversations, breaking down language barriers and facilitating smoother communication between global teams and clients.

Real-world case studies showcase how industries are already leveraging GPT-4 to their advantage.

In the e-commerce sector, businesses like Shopify use GPT-4 to generate product descriptions, optimize marketing campaigns, and automate customer interactions. This has not only improved efficiency but has also helped reduce operational costs. Similarly, in the healthcare industry, GPT-4 assists in summarizing medical research, analyzing patient data, and even generating clinical notes, saving valuable time for healthcare professionals and improving patient outcomes.

Customizing GPT-4 for Your Needs

One of the most powerful features of GPT-4 is its ability to be customized to meet specific business or creative needs.

Customization involves fine-tuning the model to perform optimally for particular tasks, industries, or projects. By training GPT-4 on domain-specific data, you can ensure that the model understands the language and terminology unique to your field, resulting in more accurate and relevant outputs. This customization allows businesses to tailor GPT-4's responses to fit their requirements, improving overall efficiency and effectiveness.

For example, a law firm could fine-tune GPT-4 using legal documents, such as contracts, case studies, and court rulings. This would enable the model to generate legal language and advice that is consistent with the firm's style and standards. Similarly, a creative agency might train GPT-4 to produce marketing copy that speaks directly to a specific audience or generates ideas for ad campaigns that align with the brand's voice.

This level of customization makes GPT-4 an even more powerful tool for businesses looking to automate processes while maintaining a high degree of personalization.

Fine-tuning GPT-4 doesn't require deep technical expertise. OpenAI provides detailed documentation and resources that guide users through the process. Whether you're adjusting GPT-4 to generate more relevant responses or training it on a custom dataset, the process is straightforward. By leveraging fine-tuning, businesses can ensure that GPT-4 is optimized for their specific use cases, delivering more accurate and useful results.

Another way to customize GPT-4 is by adjusting its output to suit different industries. For instance, in the financial sector, GPT-4 can be trained to recognize and generate financial language, making it useful for automating reports, generating market analysis, or answering customer queries related to investments. Similarly, in education, GPT-4 can be customized to assist in generating learning materials, providing tutoring, or offering feedback on assignments. The flexibility of GPT-4 ensures that it can be adapted to fit the needs of virtually any industry, making it a versatile tool for organizations across the board.

Harnessing GPT-4's API

GPT-4's true potential is fully realized when it is integrated into your systems through the OpenAI API. The API acts as a bridge between GPT-4 and your applications, allowing you to send prompts to the model and receive high-quality text responses. This integration opens up a world of possibilities for businesses, as it enables them to embed GPT-4's capabilities directly into their workflows, websites, and products.

To get started, you simply need an API key from OpenAI, which grants you access to GPT-4's powerful language model.

Once integrated, you can use the API to automate tasks, generate content, answer customer queries, or even perform data analysis, all within the applications you're already using. For instance, you can integrate GPT-4 into your customer service platform to provide AI-driven support, or use it to automate content generation within your content management system.

The OpenAI API is designed to be user-friendly, with detailed documentation that makes it easy to connect GPT-4 to your existing systems. Whether you're working with a simple website or a complex enterprise system, the API can be customized to meet your needs. Developers can easily adjust the settings to control the tone, length, and structure of the generated text, ensuring that GPT-4 fits seamlessly into the way you do business.

In addition to its simplicity and flexibility, the API provides businesses with the scalability to meet growing demands.

As your business expands, the API allows you to increase usage without worrying about performance issues. This scalability makes GPT-4 a reliable tool for companies of all sizes, from startups looking to scale up quickly to large enterprises needing to process vast amounts of data.

The ability to integrate GPT-4 via the API is one of its key strengths, allowing businesses to harness the power of AI without needing to develop their own complex language models. With just a few lines of code, companies can leverage GPT-4's full capabilities, streamlining operations and enhancing the customer experience.

Chapter 3: Ethical AI – Navigating the Responsibilities

As artificial intelligence continues to evolve and become more integrated into our daily lives, the ethical considerations surrounding its use are becoming increasingly important. GPT-4, as one of the most advanced AI models available, holds immense potential to change the way we interact with technology, but this power comes with significant responsibility. As we explore the role of AI in society, it is crucial to understand the ethical challenges that arise and how we can navigate these issues to ensure AI is used in a fair, transparent, and accountable manner.

The Importance of Ethics in AI

The development and deployment of AI technologies, including GPT-4, must be guided by a strong ethical framework that emphasizes fairness, transparency, and accountability.

These principles ensure that AI systems are not only effective but also responsible and trustworthy. **Fairness** in AI is about ensuring that the model does not discriminate against individuals or groups based on factors such as race, gender, or socioeconomic status. GPT-4, like other AI models, learns from vast datasets that often contain biases present in society. If left unchecked, these biases can be reflected in the model's outputs, perpetuating harmful stereotypes or reinforcing existing inequalities.

Transparency is another cornerstone of ethical AI. It's essential that the workings of AI systems, including how they make decisions and generate responses, are clear and understandable to the people who use them. When GPT-4 is used in critical applications, such as healthcare or finance, transparency becomes vital to ensure users can trust the system's outputs.

If a model's decision-making process is opaque, it can lead to questions about its reliability and fairness, and undermine public trust in AI technologies.

Accountability refers to the responsibility that developers, organizations, and users have in ensuring that AI systems are used appropriately and ethically. If an AI system causes harm—whether through biased outcomes or incorrect decisions—there must be mechanisms in place to hold those responsible accountable. Ensuring accountability in the development and use of GPT-4 means that developers need to take proactive steps to identify and mitigate risks, such as harmful outputs or potential misuse of the technology.

One of the significant risks associated with AI is its ability to **perpetuate bias or misinformation**. AI systems, including GPT-4, learn from data, and if that data contains biases, the model can reflect these biases in its outputs.

For example, if GPT-4 is trained on biased data related to gender or race, it might inadvertently generate text that perpetuates stereotypes.

Additionally, GPT-4 has the potential to generate misinformation. Since the model can generate text based on patterns in the data, it might produce factually inaccurate or misleading content, especially when it lacks access to real-time or verified information. To prevent such issues, developers must carefully curate training data, implement bias detection measures, and continually refine the model to minimize harmful outputs.

Ensuring Ethical Use of GPT-4

To ensure that GPT-4 is used ethically across various industries, clear guidelines and responsible usage practices must be established. One of the primary goals should be to **align GPT-4's outputs with ethical standards**, ensuring that the content generated is appropriate, accurate, and unbiased.

For businesses, this means establishing policies for the responsible use of GPT-4 in customer interactions, content creation, and data analysis. For example, companies using GPT-4 for customer service should ensure that the responses generated by the model do not discriminate against customers or promote harmful stereotypes. This involves both fine-tuning the model to the specific context and ensuring that the training data used does not include biased or harmful language.

In industries like healthcare, where GPT-4 might be used to provide medical advice or assist with clinical decision-making, ensuring ethical use is even more critical. The guidelines for GPT-4 in these contexts should include stringent checks for accuracy, a commitment to using up-to-date and credible medical data, and clear disclaimers that AI-generated content is not a substitute for professional medical advice. Similarly, in the legal sector, GPT-4 should be used carefully to avoid generating misleading legal advice or perpetuating discriminatory practices. Here, the model would need to be trained specifically on legal texts and be monitored to ensure it adheres to the standards of fairness and accuracy required in the field.

To ensure responsible usage, developers and organizations must implement robust **monitoring and auditing mechanisms** to track GPT-4's performance and address any ethical concerns that arise. These mechanisms should involve continuous feedback loops where users report problematic outputs, and developers use that feedback to improve the model. Regular audits of the data and outputs generated by GPT-4 can help identify and address biases, inaccuracies, or other issues before they cause harm.

Legal and Societal Implications

The ethical challenges posed by AI are not just technical; they also have significant **legal and societal implications**. As AI technology becomes more integrated into sectors like healthcare, finance, and law, the legal framework surrounding its use is evolving. Governments and regulatory bodies are beginning to recognize the need for AI regulations that address issues like bias, accountability, transparency, and data privacy.

For instance, the European Union has proposed the **Artificial Intelligence Act**, a comprehensive legal framework designed to regulate high-risk AI applications. This framework aims to ensure that AI systems, including GPT-4, are developed and deployed in a way that respects fundamental rights and does not cause harm to society.

From a legal perspective, the challenges surrounding AI include determining who is responsible when an AI system causes harm. If GPT-4 is used to generate harmful or misleading information, for example, it may be unclear whether the responsibility lies with the developers, the businesses using the model, or the end-users.

Legal frameworks are working to address these questions, but they are still in their early stages. Additionally, issues like **data privacy** are central to the conversation around AI. Since GPT-4 requires vast amounts of data for training, it is essential that developers ensure compliance with privacy laws, such as the **General Data Protection Regulation (GDPR)**, which sets strict guidelines for data collection and usage.

On a societal level, the widespread use of AI models like GPT-4 has the potential to disrupt industries and shift job markets. While AI can create efficiencies and reduce costs, it can also displace jobs that were previously done by humans, especially in sectors like customer service, content creation, and data analysis. To address these challenges, society must consider how to balance the benefits of AI with the need to protect workers and ensure equitable access to the opportunities that AI presents. This could involve retraining programs for workers, discussions about AI's role in society, and the development of policies that ensure AI's benefits are shared widely.

Navigating the ethical, legal, and societal responsibilities of AI is a complex but necessary task. As GPT-4 and other AI technologies continue to evolve, it is critical that they are used in ways that are fair, transparent, and accountable. By doing so, we can ensure that AI serves the greater good and contributes positively to society.

Chapter 4: Mastering GPT-4's Fine-Tuning and Optimization

The true potential of GPT-4 lies not only in its ability to generate human-like text but also in its capacity to be fine-tuned and optimized for specific tasks and industries. Fine-tuning allows users to tailor GPT-4 to better meet their needs, whether that means generating more accurate content for a particular industry, improving the quality of customer service, or optimizing responses to specific types of prompts. This process ensures that GPT-4 can provide even more relevant, contextually aware, and high-quality outputs, making it a highly customizable and powerful tool.

Understanding Fine-Tuning

Fine-tuning is the process of taking a pre-trained model like GPT-4 and adjusting it based on a specific dataset or task.

This involves training the model further using data that is specific to a particular domain or industry, allowing GPT-4 to generate more accurate and contextually appropriate responses. The fine-tuning process typically begins by identifying the specific objectives or outcomes you want GPT-4 to achieve. Whether you're looking to generate creative writing, assist with legal research, or answer customer service inquiries, fine-tuning helps GPT-4 learn the specific language, style, and terminology used in that context.

To fine-tune GPT-4, you'll need a dataset that is representative of the domain you're working in. For example, if you're building a chatbot for the healthcare industry, you would use medical texts, such as doctor-patient interactions, medical research papers, and other relevant content, to train GPT-4. This process helps the model understand the nuances of medical language and respond more accurately to healthcare-related queries.

Similarly, if you're using GPT-4 for legal document generation, you'd fine-tune the model using legal briefs, contracts, and other legal documents, ensuring that the language and style align with the standards of the legal industry.

Fine-tuning can be achieved through a series of steps. First, the model is trained on the new, domain-specific dataset. Then, feedback is incorporated to continuously refine the model's responses. This can involve testing GPT-4 with a range of prompts and reviewing the outputs to ensure they meet the desired standards. Over time, the model becomes more specialized, generating responses that are better aligned with the task at hand.

Real-world examples of fine-tuning illustrate the power of this process. For instance, a company in the finance industry might fine-tune GPT-4 to generate financial reports or assist with investment analysis.

By training the model on historical market data and financial reports, the company can ensure that GPT-4 produces outputs that are not only factually correct but also in line with industry-specific language. In another case, a legal firm might fine-tune GPT-4 on legal case studies and contracts to improve its ability to assist lawyers in drafting documents or conducting legal research.

Advanced Prompt Engineering

Once GPT-4 has been fine-tuned for a specific task, the next step is mastering **prompt engineering**, which is the art of crafting effective prompts that guide GPT-4 to produce the desired output. While GPT-4 is powerful on its own, the quality of the prompts you provide plays a crucial role in the quality of the responses it generates.

A well-crafted prompt is clear, precise, and includes enough detail to give GPT-4 the context it needs to generate accurate and relevant responses.

Effective prompt engineering involves understanding how GPT-4 interprets the language and how to structure prompts to maximize the model's output. For instance, if you're using GPT-4 to generate a summary of a lengthy article, your prompt should clearly specify what you need from the model. You might say, "Summarize the main points of the following article in 150 words, highlighting the key arguments and conclusions." This ensures that GPT-4 understands the type of output you're expecting, making it more likely to provide a concise and accurate summary.

For more complex tasks, **chaining prompts** can be an effective strategy. This involves using multiple prompts in sequence, where each prompt builds on the previous one.

Chaining is especially useful for solving multi-step problems that require GPT-4 to maintain context and coherence throughout the process.

For example, if you're generating a business report, you might start with a prompt asking GPT-4 to generate an outline of the report's key sections. Once the outline is created, you can use additional prompts to fill in each section with relevant details. This approach allows GPT-4 to tackle complex tasks that require multiple steps of reasoning and ensures that the output remains focused and relevant.

Chaining also helps when you need to adjust the model's responses based on feedback. For instance, if the first output is too brief or lacks certain details, you can refine the model's next response by providing additional context in the subsequent prompt. This iterative process helps fine-tune GPT-4's performance and ensures that the model's outputs align with your expectations.

Optimizing GPT-4's Performance

Beyond fine-tuning and prompt engineering, optimizing GPT-4's performance is essential for ensuring it delivers high-quality results consistently. There are several strategies that can help improve GPT-4's **response time**, **accuracy**, and **contextuality**.

One of the key factors influencing GPT-4's performance is the complexity of the task at hand. For tasks that require highly specific information, GPT-4 may take longer to process and generate responses. To speed up the response time, consider breaking down the task into smaller, more manageable steps. This can make the model's job easier and allow it to generate responses more quickly. Additionally, providing clear and concise instructions in the prompt can help reduce the time spent on processing irrelevant information.

Improving **accuracy** is another critical optimization strategy. To ensure that GPT-4 generates factually correct responses, you can provide it with more specific instructions or context in the prompt.

For instance, if you need a model to generate legal advice, specifying that the information should be drawn from a particular jurisdiction or legal framework can help ensure that GPT-4 produces accurate and relevant content. Incorporating external sources, such as databases or trusted websites, can further improve the accuracy of the responses.

Contextuality is another area where optimization is key. GPT-4's ability to understand context and maintain coherence throughout a conversation or text generation is one of its most impressive features, but it requires careful handling. To optimize this, it's important to feed GPT-4 with relevant background information and ensure that each prompt includes enough context to guide the model's response. You can also use follow-up prompts to clarify the context further or adjust the tone and style of the response to match the desired outcome.

By focusing on fine-tuning GPT-4 for specific tasks, engineering effective prompts, and optimizing its performance, you can ensure that the model is delivering high-quality outputs that are aligned with your goals. These strategies allow you to leverage GPT-4's full potential, ensuring that it works effectively across a wide range of applications, from content creation and customer service to data analysis and beyond.

Chapter 5: GPT-4 for Creativity and Content Generation

The arrival of GPT-4 has opened up a world of possibilities for creative professionals and businesses alike, offering unprecedented opportunities for storytelling, art creation, music composition, and much more. GPT-4's ability to generate human-like text and adapt to various styles and contexts has made it an indispensable tool for anyone looking to harness the power of AI in creative work. By understanding how to use GPT-4 for creative purposes and content generation, professionals can enhance their work, streamline processes, and unlock new levels of productivity.

Creative Uses of GPT-4

One of the most exciting applications of GPT-4 is its ability to assist in creative endeavors like storytelling, art creation, and even music composition.

Writers, authors, and filmmakers have started using GPT-4 as a collaborative tool to brainstorm ideas, outline plots, and even write entire scenes. The model's ability to generate dialogue, describe settings, and develop character arcs makes it an excellent asset for writers facing writer's block or those looking to speed up their creative processes. By providing GPT-4 with a basic idea or prompt, writers can generate entire paragraphs or scenes that can be refined and expanded upon, ultimately helping them bring their ideas to life faster.

For artists, GPT-4's potential extends beyond just text. It can assist in brainstorming concepts for artwork, providing descriptions of abstract or complex ideas that artists can visualize and interpret. Whether you're creating digital art, illustrations, or sculptures, GPT-4 can offer creative suggestions that can inspire new pieces.

By providing prompts like "generate a description of a futuristic cityscape" or "create an image of a serene landscape with an ethereal atmosphere," artists can use GPT-4's outputs as a starting point to develop their own unique visual creations.

Music composition is another area where GPT-4 is proving to be a valuable tool. Musicians are experimenting with GPT-4 to generate lyrics, chord progressions, and even entire compositions. While GPT-4 cannot directly create audio files, it can generate textual descriptions of musical ideas that musicians can use as inspiration. For example, a musician might ask GPT-4 to "generate lyrics for a song about love and loss" or "create a melody in the key of C major with a melancholy feel." These outputs can provide a framework for musicians to build upon, accelerating the creative process and sparking new ideas.

Real-world case studies highlight the growing use of GPT-4 in creative industries.

In the world of literature, authors are using GPT-4 to generate plot ideas, character names, and even complete chapters for novels.

Some writers have reported that GPT-4 serves as a collaborative writing partner, helping them overcome creative blocks and expanding their storytelling horizons. In the field of digital art, artists are using GPT-4 to generate detailed descriptions of their ideas, which they then use as the foundation for their artwork. Similarly, musicians are using GPT-4 to develop lyrics, melodies, and even entire musical arrangements, streamlining the composition process and opening new creative avenues.

Content Generation for Business

While GPT-4's creative applications are impressive, its role in business content generation is equally transformative.

Businesses across all industries are using GPT-4 to streamline their content creation efforts, ensuring that they can produce high-quality content at scale while maintaining consistency and engagement. From writing blog posts to crafting marketing copy and social media posts, GPT-4 has become a key player in the content marketing world.

Blog writing is one area where GPT-4 shines. Content marketers are using GPT-4 to generate informative, engaging, and SEO-optimized blog posts in a fraction of the time it would take to write them manually. By providing GPT-4 with a keyword or topic, marketers can generate entire articles that are both informative and aligned with search engine optimization best practices. The model can also help with brainstorming blog topics, creating catchy titles, and structuring posts to enhance readability.

For businesses that need to produce regular blog content, GPT-4 can be an invaluable tool for scaling efforts without sacrificing quality.

Marketing copy, another critical component of business communication, can also benefit from GPT-4. Whether it's creating persuasive product descriptions, drafting email campaigns, or writing landing pages, GPT-4 can generate text that is both engaging and aligned with a brand's voice. By adjusting the tone of the prompts, businesses can ensure that the generated copy resonates with their target audience, whether they're aiming for a formal, professional tone or a more casual, friendly approach. This ability to adapt to different writing styles makes GPT-4 a versatile tool for businesses looking to connect with customers in a meaningful way.

In addition to blog posts and marketing copy, GPT-4 can also play a crucial role in generating **product descriptions** and **social media posts**.

For e-commerce businesses, GPT-4 can create compelling, SEO-friendly product descriptions that highlight key features and benefits. The model can also generate social media content, from catchy headlines to full posts, allowing businesses to maintain an active online presence without spending hours crafting each post manually. By automating the creation of product listings and social media content, businesses can focus their energy on other critical aspects of their operations.

For businesses that need to scale their content production efforts, GPT-4 is an invaluable resource. With its ability to generate high-quality text at scale, companies can quickly produce large volumes of content without needing a team of writers to handle the workload. Whether you're creating articles, social media posts, or email newsletters, GPT-4's efficiency and adaptability allow businesses to maintain a consistent flow of content without compromising on quality.

Furthermore, by using GPT-4 to automate repetitive tasks like generating product descriptions or drafting initial content drafts, businesses can free up time for their teams to focus on more strategic and creative work.

The benefits of using GPT-4 for content generation extend beyond just efficiency and volume. The model's ability to learn from past content and adapt to different styles and tones ensures that businesses can maintain a consistent brand voice across all their content. Whether you're producing a formal white paper or a casual social media post, GPT-4 can help businesses create content that aligns with their unique brand identity, ensuring that all communication remains cohesive and on-message.

Chapter 6: Business Transformation with GPT-4

GPT-4 is not just a tool for content generation or creative pursuits—it's a transformative asset for businesses looking to streamline their operations, improve customer service, and enhance decision-making. As businesses face increasing pressure to optimize efficiency, reduce costs, and deliver better customer experiences, leveraging AI technologies like GPT-4 has become a game-changer. With its ability to generate human-like text, understand context, and adapt to various tasks, GPT-4 can play a pivotal role in modernizing business practices and driving innovation.

GPT-4 as a Business Tool

Businesses today are constantly seeking ways to streamline operations, reduce inefficiencies, and increase productivity.

GPT-4 offers a powerful solution to these challenges by automating tasks, improving workflows, and facilitating better decision-making. For example, GPT-4 can be integrated into internal systems to automate routine administrative tasks, such as managing emails, generating reports, and drafting internal communications. By offloading these time-consuming tasks to GPT-4, businesses can free up valuable time and resources, allowing employees to focus on more strategic and creative endeavors.

One of the most significant advantages of GPT-4 is its ability to improve **customer service**. Traditional customer service models rely heavily on human agents, leading to long response times and inconsistent service.

GPT-4, however, can be deployed as a conversational agent capable of handling a wide range of customer inquiries—everything from simple questions to more complex troubleshooting issues.

Using GPT-4-powered chatbots, businesses can offer 24/7 customer support, respond to queries instantly, and provide personalized assistance without the need for human intervention. This not only improves customer satisfaction but also reduces operational costs by minimizing the need for a large customer service team.

Another area where GPT-4 can make a significant impact is in **decision-making**. With its ability to process large amounts of data quickly and generate insightful analysis, GPT-4 can assist businesses in making informed decisions. By integrating GPT-4 with internal business systems, companies can generate detailed reports, conduct SWOT analysis (Strengths, Weaknesses,

Opportunities, Threats), and even predict future trends based on historical data. This ability to analyze data and provide actionable insights is especially valuable for managers and executives who need to make critical business decisions with confidence. GPT-4's capacity to simulate different scenarios and evaluate potential outcomes allows businesses to plan ahead and stay agile in the face of uncertainty.

Real-world examples demonstrate the success of businesses that have already embraced GPT-4 to improve their productivity. For instance, in the e-commerce industry, companies are automating their product descriptions, customer interactions, and inventory management using GPT-4. Shopify, for example, has incorporated GPT-4 to help merchants generate product descriptions automatically, freeing up time for marketing and customer engagement efforts.

Similarly, companies in the financial sector are using GPT-4 to automate tasks such as report generation and market analysis, enabling them to make more timely and informed decisions.

GPT-4 in Marketing and Customer Engagement

Marketing and customer engagement are two areas where GPT-4 can truly shine, enabling businesses to create personalized experiences, build stronger brand identities, and reach their target audience more effectively. With its deep understanding of language and context, GPT-4 can be used to generate personalized content that resonates with specific segments of customers. Whether it's crafting personalized emails, creating product recommendations, or generating tailored offers, GPT-4 can help businesses connect with customers on a more individual level.

One of the key benefits of using GPT-4 in **marketing** is its ability to create **targeted**

advertisements. By analyzing customer data and preferences, GPT-4 can generate ads that speak directly to the needs and interests of different audience segments.

For example, GPT-4 can help companies create dynamic ad copy that changes based on a user's past behavior, location, or purchase history, increasing the relevance of the ads and boosting engagement. This level of personalization ensures that businesses can reach their audience with the right message at the right time, improving the overall effectiveness of their marketing campaigns.

Another way businesses are utilizing GPT-4 in marketing is by using it to **enhance social media engagement**. Social media is a critical platform for building brand awareness, engaging with customers, and driving sales. GPT-4 can generate engaging posts, create captions, and even analyze customer feedback to help businesses understand what content resonates best with their audience.

By leveraging GPT-4's ability to create compelling content quickly, businesses can maintain a consistent social media presence, which is crucial in today's fast-paced digital world.

For **customer engagement**, GPT-4's conversational capabilities can be used to build more meaningful relationships with customers. Chatbots powered by GPT-4 can have natural, intelligent conversations with customers, helping them navigate websites, answer questions, and even complete purchases. By offering a personalized experience and providing real-time assistance, businesses can enhance customer loyalty and increase conversions.

GPT-4's ability to understand and adapt to different customer needs makes it an invaluable tool for businesses looking to improve their customer experience and build long-lasting relationships.

Data-Driven Decisions with GPT-4

In today's data-driven world, making informed decisions is more important than ever, and GPT-4 is proving to be a powerful asset in this regard. By integrating GPT-4 with data analytics tools, businesses can leverage its capabilities to analyze large volumes of data, identify trends, and make more informed strategic decisions. Whether it's sales data, customer behavior patterns, or market trends, GPT-4 can process and interpret complex datasets, providing insights that would be difficult for human analysts to uncover on their own.

For example, businesses can use GPT-4 to conduct **market research**, analyzing consumer feedback, social media conversations, and competitor strategies to gain a deeper understanding of the market landscape.

GPT-4 can generate reports that summarize key trends, identify emerging opportunities, and highlight potential risks. This allows businesses to stay ahead of the competition and make proactive decisions that drive growth.

Additionally, GPT-4 can assist with **strategic planning** by simulating different business scenarios and evaluating potential outcomes. For instance, businesses can use GPT-4 to test the impact of different pricing strategies, marketing campaigns, or product launches before making any major decisions. By running multiple simulations and analyzing the results, businesses can choose the most effective approach, minimizing risk and maximizing their chances of success.

In the world of **data analysis**, GPT-4's ability to understand and generate language makes it especially valuable for businesses that need to convert raw data into actionable insights.

Instead of relying on traditional data analysis tools that require specialized knowledge, GPT-4 can interpret data and generate clear, human-readable reports that anyone in the organization can understand and use to make decisions.

By leveraging GPT-4 for data-driven decision-making, businesses can improve their agility, make better strategic choices, and ultimately drive greater success. Whether it's analyzing customer trends, predicting future demand, or evaluating the effectiveness of marketing campaigns, GPT-4's ability to process and interpret data quickly and accurately can provide businesses with a competitive edge.

Chapter 7: Overcoming Challenges and Troubleshooting GPT-4

As powerful and versatile as GPT-4 is, no AI system is without its challenges. Understanding and addressing these challenges is crucial for ensuring that GPT-4 delivers the best results. Whether you're dealing with inaccurate responses, bias in outputs, or issues with contextuality, being able to identify and fix these problems is essential for maximizing the model's effectiveness. Moreover, as businesses and organizations begin to scale GPT-4 for large-scale use, ensuring that it performs optimally becomes increasingly important.

Troubleshooting and fine-tuning GPT-4 for high-volume operations require a deep understanding of the model's capabilities and limitations.

Finally, as we work through these challenges, it's crucial to maintain ethical standards to ensure that the use of GPT-4 remains responsible and aligned with fairness and transparency.

Common Issues with GPT-4

Despite its advanced capabilities, GPT-4 can occasionally produce inaccurate responses, exhibit bias, or fail to fully understand the context of a prompt. Addressing these issues requires a proactive approach to troubleshooting and fine-tuning.

One of the most common problems businesses face when using GPT-4 is **inaccurate responses**. While GPT-4 is highly capable, it sometimes generates outputs that are either factually incorrect or irrelevant to the query at hand. This often happens when the model doesn't fully grasp the nuances of the input or when it lacks sufficient data on the topic.

To mitigate this, it's important to provide GPT-4 with clear and well-defined prompts that help guide its output. Be specific about what you're asking, and if necessary, include context or background information to ensure the response aligns with your expectations.

Another common issue with GPT-4 is **bias** in its outputs. AI models like GPT-4 learn from large datasets, and if these datasets contain biased information, the model can reflect those biases in its responses. For example, GPT-4 might inadvertently generate text that is biased towards certain demographics or perspectives. To address this, businesses and developers must focus on training GPT-4 with diverse and balanced datasets that minimize bias.

Additionally, it's important to regularly audit GPT-4's outputs for signs of bias and adjust prompts or fine-tune the model accordingly. If you're using GPT-4 for customer service or other sensitive applications, implementing safeguards to detect and correct biased responses is critical for maintaining fairness and trust.

Another issue that can arise is a **lack of context** in GPT-4's responses. GPT-4 generates text based on patterns it has learned from its training data, but it can sometimes fail to maintain consistency or fully grasp the broader context of a conversation or task. This often happens in long-form content or multi-step tasks, where the model might forget key details from earlier parts of the conversation. To overcome this, ensure that each prompt includes sufficient context and consider using prompt chaining for more complex tasks.

Breaking down long tasks into smaller, more manageable steps and providing clear instructions for each stage can also help GPT-4 maintain better continuity and relevance in its responses.

Optimizing GPT-4 for High Volume Use

As businesses scale their use of GPT-4, performance becomes a critical consideration. Running GPT-4 on a large scale can present challenges, especially when processing high volumes of data or generating large quantities of content. Optimizing GPT-4 for **high-volume use** involves both improving its performance and managing system resources effectively.

One of the first steps in optimizing GPT-4 is to **improve response time**. As the volume of queries or tasks increases, response time can slow down, impacting user experience and productivity. To improve response times, businesses can optimize the structure of their prompts to reduce complexity and make it easier for GPT-4 to process requests. Additionally, using pre-built templates or caching frequently used responses can help speed up common tasks.

Ensuring that the system hosting GPT-4 has the appropriate hardware and processing power to handle high demand is also crucial for maintaining performance.

In addition to improving speed, businesses must focus on **resource management** when scaling GPT-4. High-volume use can demand significant computational power, which can become costly if not managed effectively. One way to manage resources is by using batch processing for tasks that require large-scale generation, such as producing content for websites or generating multiple reports at once. By grouping tasks together, businesses can reduce the number of requests sent to GPT-4 and optimize processing time. Another strategy is to use **load balancing**, distributing tasks across multiple servers or systems to avoid overloading a single server.

Monitoring GPT-4's performance regularly is also key to ensuring that it's operating efficiently.

Implementing automated performance tracking tools can help identify bottlenecks and other issues in real time, allowing businesses to address problems before they impact performance. Regular updates and maintenance are also essential to ensure that GPT-4 is functioning optimally as it is integrated into larger systems and processes.

Maintaining Ethical Standards While Troubleshooting

When troubleshooting issues with GPT-4, it's essential to ensure that **ethical standards** are maintained throughout the process. As AI becomes more integral to business operations, ethical considerations must remain a top priority, especially when dealing with potential biases or inaccuracies in the model's outputs.

One way to ensure ethical use of GPT-4 while troubleshooting is by implementing **bias**

detection systems. These systems can be used to identify when GPT-4 produces biased, harmful, or inappropriate content, allowing businesses to take corrective action. Bias detection tools can also help monitor content in real-time, flagging problematic outputs before they reach the end user. It's important to build a diverse team of reviewers who can assess GPT-4's outputs from various perspectives to ensure that ethical concerns are caught early on.

Transparency is another important aspect of maintaining ethical standards. When troubleshooting GPT-4's outputs, businesses must be transparent about how the model works, how it is trained, and how it processes data. Providing users with clear information about the limitations of GPT-4 and how their data is being used helps build trust and ensures that ethical guidelines are followed. Ensuring that users understand that GPT-4's responses are generated by an AI system—not a human—can prevent misunderstandings and promote more responsible interactions with the technology.

Finally, it's crucial to implement **accountability measures** to ensure that any issues with GPT-4's outputs are addressed promptly and responsibly. This includes setting up a system for reporting and addressing problematic outputs, as well as holding developers and businesses accountable for the ethical implications of AI usage. By taking these proactive steps, businesses can ensure that they are using GPT-4 in a way that respects user rights, promotes fairness, and avoids harmful impacts.

Chapter 8: Real-World Case Studies – Success Stories with GPT-4

GPT-4 has quickly become an essential tool in a variety of industries, providing innovative solutions that improve efficiency, enhance creativity, and drive decision-making. As its capabilities continue to evolve, businesses across sectors such as healthcare, education, finance, and e-commerce are finding new ways to incorporate GPT-4 into their operations. These real-world case studies highlight the diverse applications of GPT-4 and offer valuable insights into how businesses can harness its potential to transform their processes and achieve better outcomes.

Industry-Specific Applications

The potential of GPT-4 to transform industries is immense.

One of the most prominent areas where GPT-4 is making an impact is in **healthcare**. In this industry, time is often of the essence, and efficiency is paramount.

GPT-4 is being used to assist doctors and medical professionals by automating routine tasks such as summarizing patient records, generating diagnostic reports, and even helping with research. For instance, a healthcare provider might use GPT-4 to analyze medical journals and generate summaries of the latest research findings, saving researchers valuable time. GPT-4 is also used to assist with patient communication, providing real-time responses to common patient queries, improving the patient experience while relieving staff from answering repetitive questions.

By automating administrative tasks, GPT-4 helps healthcare professionals focus on delivering high-quality care.

In the **education** sector, GPT-4 is revolutionizing how learning materials are created and personalized for students.

Educators can use GPT-4 to generate study guides, quizzes, and tailored educational content that meets the specific needs of individual learners. GPT-4 can also serve as a virtual tutor, answering students' questions and helping them understand complex subjects in real-time. A university in the U.S. has successfully integrated GPT-4 into its online learning platform, where it assists students by providing instant feedback on their assignments and guiding them through difficult topics. The tool has been credited with enhancing the learning experience, providing personalized assistance, and improving student outcomes.

In **finance**, GPT-4 is used to analyze market trends, generate financial reports, and even automate customer service tasks.

A financial advisory firm, for example, has incorporated GPT-4 into its operations to automatically generate quarterly investment reports, saving analysts hours of work. The model also helps with sentiment analysis, enabling financial professionals to assess how market sentiment is evolving based on news articles, social media posts, and other public sources. By quickly processing large amounts of data and offering insights, GPT-4 enables businesses to make more informed and timely decisions.

E-commerce is another industry where GPT-4 is having a transformative impact. In this fast-paced sector, companies need to produce large volumes of content, such as product descriptions, customer reviews, and marketing materials. GPT-4 allows e-commerce businesses to generate these materials automatically, ensuring consistency in tone and quality while speeding up the content creation process.

A popular e-commerce platform recently integrated GPT-4 into its product listing process, allowing merchants to automatically generate optimized product descriptions that are SEO-friendly and engaging.

This not only saves time for merchants but also helps them scale their operations without compromising on content quality. Furthermore, GPT-4's conversational capabilities are being used to enhance customer service by providing real-time support through chatbots, improving customer satisfaction and reducing response times.

Case Studies of Companies and Individuals Using GPT-4 for Innovative Solutions

Numerous companies and individuals have successfully integrated GPT-4 into their operations to solve problems and enhance productivity.

One such case is **Shopify**, which integrated GPT-4 into its platform to assist merchants with automating product descriptions and enhancing customer service.

By leveraging GPT-4's language capabilities, Shopify has helped thousands of e-commerce businesses streamline their operations and increase sales by ensuring that product listings are well-written and SEO-optimized. The company also uses GPT-4 to provide real-time customer support, reducing wait times and providing customers with immediate answers to their queries.

In the **media** industry, GPT-4 is being used by content creators to enhance the writing process. One content creation agency, for example, uses GPT-4 to generate ideas for blog posts, articles, and even video scripts. By inputting general themes or topics into GPT-4, the team can quickly generate a range of content ideas and outlines, which they can then refine and develop further.

This has led to a significant increase in content output and reduced the time spent brainstorming ideas. In addition, GPT-4 is helping content creators automate repetitive tasks, such as generating social media captions or writing email newsletters, allowing them to focus more on strategy and creative aspects.

Another noteworthy case is **Khan Academy**, a leading educational platform that has been experimenting with GPT-4 to create personalized learning experiences for students. By using GPT-4 to provide instant feedback on assignments, answer student questions, and guide them through lessons, Khan Academy has been able to create a more interactive and engaging educational experience. Students using the platform benefit from the AI-powered tutor, which provides explanations and clarifications in real-time, helping them understand concepts that might otherwise be challenging.

Learning from Mistakes

While GPT-4 has proven to be a powerful tool, its implementation is not without challenges. In some cases, the model's outputs may not meet expectations or may lead to unintended consequences. These issues provide valuable lessons and insights into how to improve the effectiveness of GPT-4 in real-world applications.

One example is a **customer service implementation** where GPT-4 initially struggled to understand the nuances of customer inquiries. A company that integrated GPT-4 into its customer service system found that the model sometimes provided inaccurate or irrelevant answers, leading to frustration among customers. Upon closer examination, it was discovered that the model lacked sufficient context for certain customer queries, which led to misunderstandings.

The solution involved fine-tuning GPT-4 with a more comprehensive dataset that included a wider range of customer interactions, as well as adjusting the prompts to provide more context. This case highlights the importance of continuous training and fine-tuning when using GPT-4 for customer service applications, ensuring that it understands the complexities of human language and context.

Another example comes from an **e-commerce business** that used GPT-4 to generate product descriptions. While the model was effective at generating content quickly, it occasionally produced descriptions that were generic or lacked creativity, making the listings less engaging. The business learned that GPT-4 needed more specific guidelines and examples to generate high-quality descriptions. By providing more detailed prompts and using GPT-4 in conjunction with human creativity, the business was able to improve the quality of the product descriptions and create more compelling listings that resonated with customers.

These cases demonstrate the importance of **testing** and **iterating** when working with GPT-4. The model can produce impressive results, but it often requires fine-tuning and adjustments to align with specific business needs. By learning from mistakes and continuously refining the approach, businesses can improve their outcomes and ensure that GPT-4 is delivering maximum value.

Chapter 9: The Future of GPT-4 and AI Technology

The evolution of artificial intelligence, particularly with the advent of models like GPT-4, has already had a profound impact on the way we work, live, and interact with technology. As powerful as GPT-4 is, the journey of AI is far from over. As AI continues to advance, it's crucial to look ahead and understand what the future holds, not just for GPT-4 but for the broader field of artificial intelligence.

From the potential updates to GPT-4 to the societal shifts driven by AI, the coming years promise both exciting opportunities and significant challenges. To fully benefit from these advancements, individuals and businesses need to be prepared to adapt and leverage AI responsibly.

What's Next for GPT-4?

While GPT-4 is already an advanced and highly capable language model, its future iterations will likely bring even more powerful and refined capabilities. The next major version of GPT, potentially GPT-5, is expected to bring several improvements that will push the boundaries of what AI can do.

One of the key areas where GPT-5 could improve is **accuracy** and **contextual understanding**. GPT-4, although highly capable, can sometimes struggle with maintaining consistency in long conversations or complex tasks. GPT-5 could be designed to handle longer and more nuanced prompts, ensuring that it produces more coherent, contextually aware outputs across extended dialogues or tasks.

This improvement would make GPT-5 even more useful for applications in industries like customer service, content creation, and education, where long-term engagement and complex queries are common.

Another area for potential growth is **multi-modal capabilities**. While GPT-4 primarily focuses on text-based outputs, future versions of GPT may incorporate other types of data, such as images, video, or even sound, making the AI more versatile. For example, GPT-5 might be able to generate not just text but also accompanying visual content or audio, opening up new possibilities for industries like advertising, entertainment, and design.

Multi-modal AI systems could also be instrumental in fields like healthcare, where combining visual data (e.g., medical imaging) with text-based data (e.g., patient records) could improve diagnostic accuracy and provide more comprehensive insights.

Moreover, **reliability** and **safety** will continue to be a key focus in the development of future GPT models.

Ensuring that AI systems produce ethical, unbiased, and responsible outputs is crucial for maintaining public trust in AI technologies. Future versions of GPT will likely include improved mechanisms to detect and mitigate harmful or biased content. As AI becomes more integrated into critical applications—such as healthcare, legal services, and education—ensuring that the model adheres to ethical standards will be paramount.

The Future of AI in Society

The impact of artificial intelligence on society will be transformative. As AI continues to advance, it will touch every aspect of life—from the jobs people do to how industries operate and how businesses interact with their customers. AI's ability to process vast amounts of data, learn from it, and generate human-like outputs will change the way industries function, creating both opportunities and challenges.

In terms of **jobs**, AI will undoubtedly change the nature of work. While some jobs may be displaced by AI technologies, particularly those that involve repetitive tasks or manual labor, new opportunities will emerge in areas like AI development, data science, ethics, and human-AI collaboration. As businesses and governments embrace AI, there will be a growing demand for individuals who can work alongside AI, manage AI systems, and ensure they are used responsibly. For example, new roles in AI ethics and regulation are likely to become more prominent as the technology becomes more ubiquitous.

In the **global economy**, AI has the potential to increase productivity, reduce costs, and create new markets. Industries like **healthcare**, **finance**, and **education** will benefit from AI's ability to analyze data and generate insights, improving outcomes and efficiency. AI-driven innovations could lead to the creation of entirely new industries and business models, while also improving the services and products available to consumers. However, this also means that companies and nations that fail to adapt to the rise of AI risk falling behind, both economically and technologically.

Socially, the continued growth of AI could exacerbate **inequality** if access to the technology is not equitably distributed. Governments, businesses, and educational institutions will need to work together to ensure that the benefits of AI are shared broadly across society, rather than being concentrated in the hands of a few. There will also need to be a concerted effort to address the ethical implications of AI, particularly in terms of **privacy**, **data security**, and **human rights**.

Public trust in AI systems will be crucial, and ensuring that these technologies are used in ways that benefit society as a whole will be essential for their continued success.

Preparing for the AI Revolution

As we look ahead, it's clear that AI will continue to evolve and shape our world. To stay ahead of the curve and leverage AI effectively, both individuals and businesses need to adopt proactive strategies for integrating AI into their operations, workflows, and skill sets.

For **individuals**, preparing for the AI revolution means staying informed and upskilling in areas where AI is making an impact. This includes learning how to work with AI tools, understanding the basics of machine learning and data science, and developing skills in areas like critical thinking, creativity, and emotional intelligence—skills that complement AI's capabilities. Professionals who are adaptable, open to learning, and able to collaborate with AI systems will be well-positioned to thrive in an AI-driven world.

For **businesses**, staying ahead of the curve requires not only adopting AI technologies but also building a culture of innovation and adaptability. Businesses should consider how AI can be integrated into their existing operations, whether it's for automating processes, enhancing customer engagement, or improving decision-making. It's also important for businesses to focus on **AI ethics**, ensuring that the technology is used responsibly and that any risks, such as biases or privacy concerns, are addressed. Companies should also invest in **AI training programs** for their employees to ensure that their workforce is equipped to use AI tools effectively.

Ethical considerations will be at the forefront of AI development. As more businesses adopt AI, there will be increasing pressure to ensure that these technologies are used transparently and responsibly. Businesses that prioritize ethics in their AI strategies will not only foster trust with their customers but also stay ahead of regulatory changes and potential legal challenges.

The future of AI is exciting, but it also requires careful thought and preparation. Whether you're an individual looking to adapt to new technological realities or a business striving to stay competitive, understanding the trajectory of AI and how it will evolve is key to making the most of its potential. By preparing for the AI revolution, we can ensure that we harness the power of this technology in ways that benefit society, drive innovation, and improve our collective future.

Chapter 10: Becoming a GPT-4 Expert – A Path Forward

As we reach the final chapter of this exploration into the world of GPT-4, it's important to reflect on the journey of learning and mastering this powerful technology. From understanding its core functionalities to applying it in real-world scenarios, mastering GPT-4 is just the beginning. The path forward involves continuous learning, exploring advanced resources, and considering how GPT-4 can shape future career opportunities in the burgeoning field of artificial intelligence. As AI continues to evolve, there are endless possibilities for individuals and businesses to stay ahead of the curve and unlock the full potential of GPT-4.

Next Steps for GPT-4 Mastery

Mastering GPT-4 is an ongoing process, one that requires continual practice, learning, and refinement. To truly become an expert, it's important to remain committed to improving your skills and understanding the nuances of the model. The first step in this journey is to **get hands-on experience**. Regularly experimenting with different tasks and applications of GPT-4 will help solidify your understanding of how the model works and how to get the best results. Whether you're creating content, building applications, or solving complex problems, the more you use GPT-4, the more adept you'll become at leveraging its capabilities.

To further improve your skills, it's essential to dive deeper into **advanced resources**. OpenAI provides a wealth of documentation, tutorials, and guides for developers, which can help you gain a more technical understanding of how GPT-4 operates. These resources offer valuable insights into the inner workings of the model, such as training techniques, optimization methods, and advanced fine-tuning. As AI technology continues to evolve, keeping up with the latest research papers, webinars, and online courses related to GPT-4 and AI development will be crucial for expanding your knowledge base.

One of the best ways to master GPT-4 is to **collaborate with others**. Joining online communities, forums, or AI-focused groups can provide opportunities to discuss your experiences, share insights, and learn from others. Collaboration often leads to breakthroughs and new ideas, allowing you to stay ahead of the curve and discover innovative ways to apply GPT-4 in your work. Whether it's through open-source projects, hackathons, or professional networks, engaging with the broader AI community is a fantastic way to continue growing and refining your skills.

Building a Career in AI

Mastering GPT-4 can open up a world of career opportunities in the growing field of artificial intelligence. As more industries adopt AI technology, there is an increasing demand for professionals with expertise in AI, machine learning, and natural language processing. GPT-4, as one of the most powerful AI language models, provides an excellent foundation for building a career in these fields.

One of the most direct career paths that mastering GPT-4 can lead to is **AI development**. AI developers are responsible for designing, building, and maintaining AI systems like GPT-4. With a strong understanding of how GPT-4 works, you can contribute to the development of new AI models, work on fine-tuning existing systems, or even build custom applications that leverage GPT-4's capabilities.

The demand for AI developers is rapidly growing, particularly as more businesses seek to integrate AI into their operations, from chatbots and automation to advanced data analysis and creative applications.

Another career opportunity is in **data science**, where GPT-4's ability to process and analyze large amounts of data can be applied to real-world problems. As a data scientist, you could use GPT-4 to analyze trends, create predictive models, and generate insights from data. Businesses in fields like healthcare, finance, and marketing are increasingly relying on data-driven decision-making, and the need for skilled professionals who can harness the power of AI models like GPT-4 will only continue to rise.

For those interested in **AI ethics**, mastering GPT-4 can also open doors to careers that focus on ensuring AI technologies are used responsibly.

As AI becomes more integrated into society, ethical concerns regarding fairness, transparency, and bias are at the forefront. Professionals in this field work to establish guidelines, regulations, and best practices for AI development and deployment. By understanding the ethical challenges associated with GPT-4 and other AI models, you can play a critical role in shaping the future of AI technology.

Beyond development and data science, GPT-4 expertise can lead to careers in areas like **AI consulting**, **product management**, and **AI education and training**. As businesses and institutions seek to adopt AI solutions, they need professionals who can guide them through the process, help optimize their use of AI, and train their employees on how to effectively integrate AI into their work.

The possibilities are endless, and as AI continues to evolve, there will be even more career paths for those with expertise in GPT-4 and related technologies. By mastering GPT-4, you position yourself at the forefront of one of the most exciting and dynamic fields in technology today.

Concluding Thoughts

In conclusion, GPT-4 is more than just an advanced AI tool—it is a glimpse into the future of technology and how we will interact with machines moving forward. Whether you're using GPT-4 for content creation, customer service, data analysis, or innovative applications, its potential to transform industries and change the way we work is immeasurable. However, with this power comes responsibility. As we embrace AI technology, it's important to approach it with **confidence**, but also with **caution** and **responsibility**.

Ensuring that AI is used ethically, transparently, and fairly is crucial to ensuring its long-term success and positive impact on society.

By committing to continuous learning and embracing the evolving field of AI, individuals and businesses can stay ahead of the curve, harnessing the full potential of GPT-4 to drive innovation, solve complex problems, and improve lives. The future of GPT-4 and AI is bright, and those who embrace this technology will be well-positioned to shape the next wave of innovation.

The path to mastering GPT-4 is just the beginning of a journey that will lead to new opportunities, personal growth, and career advancements in the exciting world of AI. By staying curious, ethical, and proactive, you can unlock the transformative power of GPT-4 and become part of the AI revolution that is already shaping the future.

Conclusion

As we conclude this journey through the world of GPT-4, it's clear that this technology holds incredible potential to shape the future of various industries and revolutionize how we work, create, and interact with machines. From enhancing creativity and streamlining business operations to enabling smarter decision-making and improving customer experiences, GPT-4 is a powerful tool that offers endless possibilities.

However, the true value of GPT-4 lies not just in its ability to generate human-like text or automate complex tasks but in how it empowers individuals and organizations to leverage AI in a responsible, ethical, and innovative way. As with any powerful technology, it is our responsibility to ensure that GPT-4 is used ethically, transparently, and in ways that benefit society as a whole. By addressing challenges, fine-tuning approaches, and maintaining ethical standards, we can ensure that AI continues to improve lives and drive positive change.

The path to mastering GPT-4 is a journey of continuous learning, exploration, and adaptation. As AI technology evolves, those who embrace it with curiosity, confidence, and responsibility will be at the forefront of this exciting revolution. Whether you are using GPT-4 for creative projects, business innovations, or personal growth, the opportunities are vast, and the future is full of promise.

Ultimately, embracing GPT-4 means stepping into a world where the boundaries between human creativity and machine intelligence blur, opening new avenues for innovation, problem-solving, and growth. As we move forward into this AI-driven future, it is essential to remain proactive, informed, and

committed to using GPT-4 and other AI
technologies in ways that empower us all,
ensuring that the full potential of AI is
harnessed for the greater good.